Tantric Training
In the Age of Ray 7

Klaire D. Roy

Translated from the original French version by
Josée Di Sario

Printed and bound in Canada by Imprimeries Transcontinental, April 2008.

©*Tantric Training In the Age of Ray 7,* Klaire D. Roy

ISBN: 978-1-896523-64-4

© Paume de Saint-Germain Publishing
Montreal, Quebec, Canada, 2008

Registration of copyright: Second trimester 2008
National Library of Quebec
National Library of Canada

Paume de Saint-Germain Publishing©
235 Rene Levesque Boulevard East, Suite 310, Montreal, Quebec, Canada H2X 1N8
Telephone: (514) 255-8700 ~ Facsimile: (514) 255-0478
E-mail: info@palmpublications.com;
Web site: http://www.palmpublications.com

Graphic Design: E.K., Eric Mathieu, Lucie Robitaille
Page layout and typesetting: Louise Roy
Editing and proofreading: Marc Bergeron, Lisa Corbeil, Luc Lemaître, Kristiane Roy, Louise Roy, Léo-Paul Senécal

©All rights reserved. No part of this book may be reproduced in any form without permission in writing from the author, except to quote or photocopy specific passages for the purposes of group study.

English books by Paume de Saint-Germain Publishing:

The Lion's Roar – The Master from Montreal, Klaire D. Roy, 2008.

New Tantrism, Klaire D. Roy. 2008.

New Tantrism, Introductory Themes, Klaire D. Roy, 2007.

Conclave of the Cryptic 7, Klaire D. Roy, Volume I, 2007.

The Spiritual Science of Essential Yoga: Techniques of Meditation, Mantrams, and Invocations, Volume I, Sri Adi Dadi, compiled by Martine G. Fortier, 2004.

Brahman's Egg, Scriptings of the Soul in Question of Light, Volume I, Sri Adi Dadi, 1995.

French books by Paume de Saint-Germain Publishing:

Entraînement au Tantrisme dans l'Ère du Rayon 7, Klaire D. Roy, 2007.

Le Nouveau Tantrisme, Klaire D. Roy, 2007.

Thèmes d'Introduction au Nouveau Tantrisme, Klaire D. Roy, 2006.

Le Rugissement du Lion de Montréal, Klaire D. Roy, 2006.

Le Projet des 7, Tome I, Ekeena Iothe, 2004.

Voyage au cœur de l'âme – La Voie de la Connaissance, Tome 2, 2003.

La Voie... à pleine Voix – Inspiré de l'enseignement de Sri Adi Dadi, 2002.

Dadi Jyoti, L'Éveil d'une Lumière Infinie, Bhai Bibi Mataji, 2001.

Namaskar – Lettres à Dadi (24 avril 1994 - 26 janvier 1999), Tome II, Bhai Bibi Mataji, 2001, second edition in print.

La science des asanas-mudras – techniques dhyanam, dynamiques et invocatoires, Tome I, enseignées par Sri Adi Dadi, 2001.

La Voie de la Connaissance – Quelques percées de Lumière inspirées de l'enseignement de Sri Adi Dadi, Tome 1, 1999.

Foudre Divine... Parfum de Rose, Josée D. Senécal, second edition in print, 1995.

Namaskar à mon Guru, Tome I. Bhai Bibi Mataji, second edition in print, 1995.

Forthcoming books in English:

Conclave of the Cryptic 7, Volume II, Klaire D. Roy.

Namaskar – Letters to Dadi (April 24, 1994 - January 26, 1999) Volume II, Bhai Bibi Mataji.

The Spiritual Science of Essential Yoga: Techniques of Meditation, Mantrams, and Invocations. Volume II. Sri Adi Dadi. Compiled by Martine G. Fortier.

Forthcoming books in French:

La science des asanas-mudras – techniques dhyanam, dynamiques et invocatoires, Tome II. Enseignées par Sri Adi Dadi.

Le Projet des 7, Tome II, Klaire D. Roy.

Forthcoming books in Russian:

Conclave of the Cryptic 7, Volumes 1 and 2, Klaire D. Roy.

Table of Contents

Prologue 1

Foreword 3

Introduction 5

Man's Ignorance 7

The Destiny of Form Depends on Man 9

Man Must Conquer the World of Matter 13

Technological Evolution: An Irresistible Trap . . .15
for Man

The Effects of the Descent of Ray 19

The Appropriate Use of the Influence of Ray . . .21

The Complexity of Man .23

Man's Suffering 27

Suffering Must be Authentic 31

The Four Stages of Suffering 35

The Monad's Suffering .39

The Sense of Separateness Must Disappear 41

The Origin of Suffering .45

The New Psychology 49

Doubt 51

Man, the Source of His Own Suffering 53

Personal Commentaries by the Tibetan 55

Life Conditions on Earth 57

- Existential Doubt Experienced by Man 59
- Occult Obedience 61
- Man's Instinct 63
- The Different Planes of Consciousness 65
- Physical-Etheric Plane 67
- The Emotional Plane 71
- The Sub-Planes of the Emotional Body 75
- The Mental Plane 79
- Concrete and Subtle Atmic Planes 83
- The Monadic Plane 87
- The Monadic Vehicle 89
- The Principle 93
- The Principle linked to this planet 97
- The Physical Brain 101

Prologue

Suffice it for you to know that I am Tibetan of origin and that my teachings aim to be more occult than mystical, since my work consists of awakening mankind so that he may become the bearer of his divine aspect. Mankind is not meant to live in ignorance. He is meant to become a conscious Light evolving within the cosmic plan of our planet. My task therefore, consists in transmitting to mankind the teachings that will allow him to become a free being, conscious of who he is and of what he is being called upon to become.

Djwhal Khul, The Tibetan

Foreword

This book has been transmitted by the one we call the Tibetan. Themes on tantric training under the influence of Ray 7 are herein explored. It in no way casts doubt on that which has already been written on the subject. However, it does allow us to cast a new look on a subject that is as old as the world. Since this book was dictated by D.K. in a sporadic fashion from January 21 to July 22, 2004, the treated subjects are not laid out in alphabetical order, but in the sequence in which they were received.

Klaire D. Roy

Introduction

Tantra is a source of Joy and a source of suffering. Trying to understand it intellectually demands a super-Human effort, since the understanding of Tantra does not depend on the brain although it is related to it. The masters of tantrism are men who have been able to develop the faculty of living without utilising their brain, in order that divine intuition could instill itself. Tantra "lights" the path instead of encumbering it. It removes accumulated dust that represents old thoughts and allows the penetration of an exceptional fresh breeze. Tantra, like the wind, cannot be captured nor imprisoned. It is free in its manifestation. We can but feel the ensuing effect of its transformation. Tantra is an enigma that few can understand in its totality. It reveals itself as a complete "map" towards illumination of which the paths are rigged and hidden, in order to allow only those pure and sensitive of heart to travel those roads without obstruction. Those of impure heart cannot but get lost in the meanderings of the illusions of the paths and roads they attempt to undertake. To take up the "road" in Tantrism in no way indicates that we are on the "Path". The presence of a Guide becomes a necessity. He will "know" how to distinguish true from false by bypassing the mind too often seduced by the illusion of evolution, which the artificial intelligence of the brain procures.

Man's Ignorance

The human aspect of this humanity that is constantly evolving and is called upon to further develop itself according to several points, since the human being has not yet understood his role and has not yet developed his full potential. The maximum utilization of the capacity of his seven bodies will become imperative during the reign of the seventh kingdom.

Man is ignorant, and in his ignorance he forgets to perfect that which constitutes him. He abuses it, uses it without truly recognizing who he is, a being designed to evolve and participate in the grand cosmic plan that encompasses several universes. God, that is that which we call God without knowing Him nor understanding Him, in His infinite wisdom, has allowed man a certain freedom within a restrained space for expressing his capacity to live out his experiences.

Man, as far as his authentic being is considered, is not free in his essence; he is linked to the invisible and indivisible thread that makes up his universe and that is part of the great brotherhood of diverse units that make up the area of activity of this God who has created us to serve Him through his own cause. God is not unique, nor the only one. He is part of an amalgam of entities so evolved that it is impossible for us to even perceive the shadow of their existence.

The Destiny of Form Depends on Man

Man has always been alone as he journeyed on the path. He has understood and suffered through this experience that has not allowed him to perfectly accomplish his destiny up until now. Will he succeed?

Within his hands lies the answer that he alone has known how to forge and to which he alone is qualified to answer. A buckle must be buckled , the cycle complete, in terms of his humanity in form. Man's form remains a stage through which his Spirit must journey. He cannot free himself of this form without having understood its meaning and importance. He can only free himself of it once he will have accomplished the destiny of form, which depends on his own destiny.

Form must be perfected to its maximum. Each cell and each molecule has an obligation to be filled to its full capacity, with divine light that burns within without having attained his full potential. It is incumbent upon Man to light up, by his own Consciousness, the iridescent light of each atom that shapes his own form and that of others. It is his responsibility. He must extricate himself from the darkness of form by illuminating the form. It is the only way, the only possible exit for him.

Whether man lives here, in Tibet or elsewhere, the challenge remains the same: to become one's own guiding light for his own knowledge and own understanding. Man must first "Know" before understanding, so that when man will "Know", he will "know" that he Knows and his "understanding" of that which he will "Know" will become "Knowledge" allowing his Consciousness to "Know".

The Master must light up his student's Consciousness through the knowing of knowledge, which must grow in the student and the disciple just like a young oak tree on the edge of a precipice that "knows" that it exists, "knows" that it will become big despite the difficulties and "knows" that the immensity that surrounds him rubs elbows with the emptiness and the fullness that forge the roots of his knowing.

The young tree aspires to become much bigger. It is the same with the Consciousness that must grow before felling into an emptiness that will free it from the formal world of form; from this structure that has allowed it to learn and to understand an aspect of itself essential to its accomplishment.

Man Must Conquer the World of Matter

It is still difficult to remove the Consciousness of man from his unconscious and his ignorance. Man has always been hypnotized by the world of matter and by the bonds of attachment created towards this matter.

The world of matter has allowed man to master and to conquer the molecular density of which all matter is composed, including his own physical body. Matter has not only served as an anchor, it has allowed him to increase his capacity to operate in worlds in which apparent difficulties were in fact challenges that he had to master in order to increase his vibratory capacity in relation to the tests that await him on the path.

Matter has reinforced man's desire to free himself of it, since this force of attachment that holds him back hides in fact the method to free himself of that which impedes his destiny.

Conquering the world of matter prepares him to conquer his own power that is asleep within him. Matter or the freedom from the attraction of the world of matter is the first important step of man in his immediate becoming.

With the advent of Ray 7, those who have already begun to work on freeing themselves of the bonds to matter will see certain difficulties ironed out, since their Consciousness will have developed the capacity for listening to the high vibrations coming forth from their higher bodies and the occult spheres that populate their lives.

Technological Evolution: An Irresistible Trap for Man

Comfort and ease of living will be exceptional in the coming age, and living in the world of matter will be even more magnetic, since the magic of technological evolution will do its work by creating irresistible forms allowing man to be distracted.

Those who will wish for more difficult physical lives, in order to perfect their evolution, will deliberately choose to go and live in other systems or planets where life conditions will be more difficult.

For those who will wish to languish on the path, this new comfort will become a beneficial trap that will prevent their spiritual evolution and their Liberation. For them, the world of matter will become a magical prison from which they will find it difficult to extricate themselves.

Therefore man must adjust himself starting now, for that which is coming and to observe this technological future with a detached eye as to the effect this new comfort will have on his life and his evolution.

The more Consciousness awakens, the more material comfort becomes a glimmer from which it is easy to escape. On the contrary, the more we remain unconscious, the more the challenge is a major one, and the more that difficulties will seem almost impossible to resolve.

I feel sorry for those who will not have opened up their Consciousness to that which is occurring and who will not have undertaken a serious work of detachment towards that which they believe to be and to that which they believe they should be. The illusion of what they believe to be will prove to be as great as their unconscious.

In the coming centuries everything will be technologically possible. The conscious man will make the parallel between his evolution and the technological evolution. He will see that everything is possible and accessible. Instant awakenings will be frequent among those who will have already begun to sprout their inner seed that will allow them to attain their full realization. Beware those who will not have begun to grow this seed or who will not have seeded it. Their lives will be satisfying on the physical level, but execrable from the point of view of the inner life. With Ray 7, there will be waves of suicide among those who have little awareness and who will feel, without understanding, the emptiness of their lives.

The Effects of the Descent of Ray 7

Ray 7 will contribute much to the evolution of mankind on the different physical, technological, psychological and mental planes. The awakening of the senses will be at its apogee, and better control will be demanded on the part of the disciples. It is for this reason that our wish is that the majority of humanity quickly achieve the second initiation, because the world of the senses will be devastating for those who will have become slaves and who will not know how to apply intelligence.

There will be abuses on many levels that will lead to chaos from the psychological point of view, because there will be too much physical comfort and too much permissiveness in all areas of life. Some will lose themselves in the ease of the senses, others will feel lost.

Thankfully some will experience an evolution of their Consciousness, which will quickly lead them to the awakening. Contact with the other worlds will be more open, easier, and fiction will become a palpable reality. Man will journey to different dimensions just as he will journey to different planetary or galactic systems.

Ray 6 allowed man to better focus on the astral or emotional plane. He must now apply intelligence to all of this.

Ray 7 is colder but more orderly. It will guide the sincere seeker by impressing within his magnetic fields, sonar resonances derived from other planetary systems and this will allow him to accomplish phenomenal work on all aspects of his being. Bodies will be longer, and man will easily attain seven feet (2 meters) in height, reflecting the manifestation of this Ray.

Bodies will be more beautiful, and the brain in its system of thinking will be more orderly and efficient. There will not be a loss of time in choosing the methods for awakening Consciousness. A precise science that will result from the art of invocation will allow an increase in the efficiency of inner work. Man will no longer seek the already established link with his Soul, but will seek contact with the Monad.

The Appropriate Use of the Influence of Ray 7

Ray 7 will bring its good and its bad aspects for the evolution of man. Ray 6 has allowed man to get close to the heart, which is not yet open among most people. Ray 7 will give the heart an intelligence to the person who will have known how to begin to open his or her heart, otherwise it will bestow a cruel reality.

Man must learn how to express energy without using force, except in exceptional cases in which the Soul intervenes for the good of all. These cases are rare and, as mentioned, exceptional. Ray 7 will bring a more just vision to man regarding certain aspects of his life all the while creating certain mirages that will obscure this same vision. Blind beauty creates needs, dependencies that are not necessary. It can make one happy or a slave depending on the polarization of man.

The era of Ray 7 will bring cultural exchanges among different countries, allowing the beginning of homogeneity to the human race. Man will become unique in his expression while keeping a part that is original and proper to his Soul, which will tint his personality with a note that will be personal and distinctive without being separative.

Children will play a major role in the future of humanity. Their education will begin very early so that their personalities can be perfected, which will need to be solid in this world of the senses in which everything will make sense or lose sense. The child who will have a good framework and be well educated will become a tool for extraordinary service, and will be able to help those who are lost to better center themselves and understand themselves.

The next 100 years will see only one out of three children receive an adequate education adapted to the era that is upon us. The others will be lost and will experiment lives of difficult experiences where violence will skim ignorance due to their unconsciousness in regards to the power of Ray 7 that will affect their destiny. This Ray, which is of an extraordinary beauty, will be a Pandora's box for these children that we will qualify as Souls in distress during the period of their existence in which their energetic structure will not be adequately supported.

The Complexity of Man

Subduing the world of matter is a major challenge, which humanity will try to accomplish under the reign of Ray 7. At present, man lives rather in good company with the world of matter, which still dominates him almost at all levels.

In the next century many will have gone past the first stage by succeeding in their first initiation, which will allow them to take a look at certain aspects of themselves of which they had no inkling. The opening of the heart will occur among many, and this will create adjustments at several levels, but also conflicts. The heart and intelligence will be a team or will become enemies.

It isn't easy to conceive of man without duality, since man is duality and multiplicity. He is dual in his material existence, and multiple in his essence, which creates discomfort and incomprehension in his vision of things.

All is complex, and only simplicity of vision will allow a true adjustment of the bodies and the energy of man in order that his destiny be accomplished, which will be an accomplishment of the law regulating this part of the universe in which we are not alone.

Man's complexity makes it such that he is like a diamond that, because of its different facets, shines the different faces of God who is not unique but as diversified as man can be. We have no idea of His greatness since we are unconscious of our own.

We are noble beings who have come from elsewhere and who possess the potential to accomplish that which the Masters call God's work comprised within the diversified "Unique".

Within man's nature is the beginning of his ascension towards his destiny and his task is complex since his Spirit is complex. He can accomplish much with very little. Man can survive among very difficult conditions, which is very uncommon in other worlds in which entities of all sorts evolve.

Man is strong in his Consciousness and this strength guides him towards good or towards evil. His anger can destroy, in just a few seconds, that which will have taken years to construct (a civilization, a nation...), because even if he believes the contrary, man does not have any real limits. He will have to learn to grow in wisdom if he does not wish to auto-destruct before the end of the next century.

Man's Suffering

In his desire to advance, man sometimes forgets the middle ground and enters worlds where suffering takes over a large part of his energy. He allows himself to be distracted by non-essential issues to his apprenticeship.

Suffering isn't always necessary, but understanding its true source, is. All originates from the all and everything returns to the all, whether it be good or not. The worlds that intermingle in the auric field of man pushes him to pursue the great dream desired and produced by God Himself who desires nothing but wants everything.

God's dream is neither materialistic, nor astral, mental, or causal, but encompasses all the worlds in which man evolves somehow or other, despite the obstacles that he creates for himself and despite the obstacles that are created for him. Everything proceeds from the beginning and everything returns to this source when the cycle is complete.

Man's suffering can purify him and destroy him by destroying those non-essential and non-definitive parts within and that encompass him.

In the coming age, man's evolution will include certain important stages that will allow him to render justice to the grandeur of the Soul that inhabits him. One of the first steps will be the forgetting of who he is, of what he has always been and what he believed himself to be.

He will go through various tests that will allow him to see and recognize the illusion of his past vision in regards to what he tried to express with his personality not yet perfected in the expression of his Soul. He will learn, thanks to these tests, to discern the true from the false, to deepen the knowledge of what he is in terms of the different facets that constitute him.

This will not be achieved without tears and cries that will resonate to the confines of the Soul that will listen to the resonance of these cries in order to discover the perfect note that will allow man to pursue his destiny to link with the Monad.

This road, littered with obstacles that cause that which needs to be worked on and corrected to re-surface, will become a road similar to the Calvary, a road allowing wisdom to unfold in the deepest parts of one's being, the entity called "man".

Ray 7 will allow the one that will be well guided to free himself of certain concepts that up until now were necessary for the opening of the heart, but not essential to the opening of the Spirit. He will learn to work with these two aspects while attempting not to lose himself in the illusory forms that this very same Ray will create in the form of mirages that will prevent one from having a just vision of things, as was the case with Ray 6.

These mirages are necessary and their purpose, because they do have a purpose, is to lead man to precise points in his Consciousness in order to allow him later on to go further than the limit that the mirage brings.

The mirage is the effect that man must outwit in order to continue on his path towards the perfection of his being.

Suffering Must be Authentic

The pearl that gushes forth from the process of suffering has no value if the suffering is not authentic or simply egoic. Suffering that does nothing but polish the surface of the ego only accentuates the faults that need work.

An authentic suffering is often silent and brings in its wake clarifications on the depths that constitute one's being. It cannot be cultivated. It is simply experienced, allowing the freeing of memories that are non-essential to the evolution of Consciousness.

Consciousness does not suffer. It lives through various experiences engendered by the desire to live, here on this planet, the conditions linked to human nature. Man is not perfect, but he can become so by working at it, and by looking within himself in order to better understand himself through the thousand facets that constitute him.

Man does not understand himself because he has never really tried to understand himself. He has drifted on the surface of things, trying to grab the maximum of useless knowledge for the awakening of Consciousness. This vision must change and will change in the coming centuries, because the survival of the human race depends upon this awakening.

If man does not begin to better understand himself, it will come to the point where he will destroy himself as well as the human race and the entire planet. The result will be a heavy karma for those lazy and egotistical Souls in incarnation and they will have to pay by repairing elsewhere the destruction that similar beings will have caused.

We hope that the human race, with the advent of this new reign, will react positively to this new energy that will allow a deeper clarity regarding knowledge that will be used in a more just fashion for the awakening of mankind.

The awakening must occur "en masse" in the next centuries. Many will simultaneously cross this threshold because time is of the essence and the future of humanity depends upon it. Those who will not have been able to face this reality will wander about in the maze of Consciousness in which they will feel lost.

This is what will happen with too much energy on this planet; it will bring to these unfortunate ones more unhappiness, because they will not have been able to face that which they need to become. Therein lies the importance of things, looking ahead with the firm intention not of changing things, but to change oneself in order to perfect evolution that asks nothing but to express itself through us.

The Four Stages of Suffering

The fullness of Spirit cannot be attained but by different stages of suffering linked to the personality as well as to the Soul.

<u>The first stage</u> concerns the efforts made by the personality to maintain his status quo, which it believes to be primordial to its survival. The personality likes to suffer because the energy channelled by this suffering gives it a tiny conviction that it is alive. The personality needs strong stimulations in order to believe in its existence. It suffers and makes others suffer. It does not know how to live otherwise.

This stage is experienced primarily before the first initiation, since the opening of the heart has not yet taken place, all is centered on the self and not on the needs of others. This stage affects man up until the fourth initiation because the memories of suffering experienced in past lives and encrusted in his nadis regularly re-surface.

<u>The second stage</u> that begins delicately after the first initiation includes a suffering that is inclined towards an awakening of Consciousness. The personality begins to suffer because of its suffering. It knows that it exists and desires a better existence. Its suffering becomes sharper and uncomfortable.

The personality often confuses these two stages of suffering and unconsciously the Soul is subjected to them one after the other. The personality oscillates between its love for suffering and its desire to suffer in an efficient manner in order to liberate itself from this suffering.

There is no escape from suffering, it is a gift or an ordeal depending on the vision of the individual who undergoes it. He can be the victim or he can see it as a liberating factor that will lead him towards a balance between his personality and his Soul.

<u>The third stage</u> of suffering comes from the Soul who awakens to its own pain at not being able to fuse with the personality. There is a battle that takes place between the Soul and the personality starting after the second initiation. The pain felt by the Soul is a sharp pain but healthy. In this suffering exists a joy that is not perceptible in the other two stages. This joy comes from the fluttering of the Soul's wings that struggles to send bursts of light towards the personality that can now tap into them.

This stage is important, since there finally is communication between the personality and the Soul.

The fourth stage concerns pain experienced by the Soul which desires to fuse with the Spirit or the Monad. It knows that the work is just beginning and that it will have to go through the sacrifice of its personality that it will offer on the altar of its Consciousness in order to better serve and fill its atomic space with a beginning of Monadic light that is much more circular and occult than its own.

The Monadic light is marked by a circular energy that prevents it from stagnating and that makes it perpetually evolve. The Monad circulates continually and oscillates between its worlds and ours. It does not really belong to our world, and its suffering, which concerns the following stage, comes from its connection to our plane of existence when man, who is attached to the Monad, awakens to its vibration and captures a part of its energy, which must now descend and adapt to an energy that is gross because it is linear.

The Monad's Suffering

The Monad's suffering has nothing in common with our suffering because it is neither egoic nor egotistical. It has nothing to do with the emotional body of man. It tolerates its state without however vibrating emotionally to this state. The pain that is felt comes from the Soul (linked to man), which attempts to adjust itself to the Monad but with difficulty. This lack of adjustment creates vibrations that affect, in a sense, the Monad who feels its jolts as a discordant note in its condition.

This temporarily breaks the harmony that reigns within it (the Monad) and provokes oscillations felt beyond its condition. These oscillations are not emotional, neither mental, they are simply frequential vibrations that contain the "all" while being "nothing".

The Monad is a tiny part of that which we call God; it contains Him without however containing

Him. It vibrates to its own note, which is in fact just a simple note lost in a symphony that never stops. Each system or galaxy possesses its own symphony. Each planet of the same system is simply a part of the score of the same symphony.

Understanding the suffering of the Monad is an impossible task for the ordinary man, but an easy task for the man of good or for the one who has succeeded in going beyond the stage of having a grip on the Soul, or that the Soul has on him. Man must one day free himself of this grip in order to pursue his path beyond the Soul, and then beyond the Monad which is but a link in the chain of our evolution.

The Sense of Separateness Must Disappear

Human destiny will continue as long as there are men ready to perfect their evolution on Earth.

The reign of Ray 7 will bring huge progress on all levels, including that of love and the understanding of this love. A higher sensitivity will ensue, since the fusion of the head with the heart will become possible, and man will realize that it is in "the order of things" and that everything must be so.

Therefore there will no longer be a sense of separateness between the heart and the Soul as was the case during the reign of Ray 6. A constant stream of energy will circulate between these two poles that will become one. Apprenticeship methods will change as will approaches in meditation. Man will no longer meditate, at least not in the same fashion. He will no longer be passive, waiting to be saved;

surely, he will save himself by more scientific methods, but more efficiently.

A new discipline will be born, more fluid but more dense in its approach. He will no longer do anything without first having reflected on the impact of his actions. All will be calculated in the good sense of the term. It will not be scientific but methodical, and this will give it all its efficiency.

Man will realize that he is not alone and will act accordingly. A great kinship will reign in certain corners of the planet in which man will function in this sense. Where man will not have understood and will act in opposition to Ray 7 or in its negativity, there will reign chaos that will put the planet in danger. We have already discussed this and will talk about this again later. The awakening of man must happen quickly, because the advent of Ray 7 will destroy, in its passage, many things that up until now impeded the accomplishment of man's task on Earth.

In this new era, which will bring clarity or obscurity depending on the case, the disciple will have had to acquire a solid base within himself allowing the work of the Soul and of Spirit to accomplish itself.

This task will not be easy for him because he will be solicited on all sides, as much by the material world that will have become increasingly more attractive because of its perfection, and as much by his circle of friends and family who will not necessarily have undertaken the disciple's path and who will judge him.

There will be an interesting duality that will strengthen the sincere man on the path but that will destroy the weak man who will fall into addictions and who will have a very difficult time getting out of them.

Man's potential is immense and it will grow accordingly. Those who have undertaken a serious spiritual path will progress rapidly and will experience moments of extraordinary ecstasy. They will quickly realize that these moments of ecstasy are illusions, but they will appreciate them, thanking their Soul for giving them this moment of temporary respite.

The era of Ray 7 will bring methods of rejuvenation at all levels (physical as well as etheric), which will allow man to live longer and more efficiently. He will therefore be even more responsible for his psychic and atmic maturity. He will have to increase his power within himself in order to increase his capacity to receive the energies of the Soul that will become increasingly stronger and present.

The Origin of Suffering

The true origin of suffering isn't related to the noble truths enunciated by the Buddha himself. It is in fact more occult, more complex; since the precepts of the Buddha apply to the personality, whereas suffering holds a more occult goal, more complex and that encompasses even the Soul and the Monad.

Souls evolving on this planet know full well that the suffering experienced here is but a prelude to greater suffering that will allow the Monad to experiment its own awakening linked to another dimension beyond its concern.

The Monad who has suffered can, because of its energy and thanks to its origin, carry in space and time an energy that will allow it to adapt itself and to understand in a global and concrete way, other species and the limitations to which they are subjected.

The origin of suffering does not come from unquenched desires but from the absorption and regulation of germ atoms that characterize our evolution. This suffering tints the atom in such a way that we are easily recognized elsewhere as being high-spirited fighters for justice and where balanced laws govern the universe.

We thus become by this very fact, excellent diplomats able to converse and manage thanks to this precious knowledge gained from the study of all the illusory facets of pain that have nothing to do with authentic suffering of the Soul and of the Spirit, which are neither temporal, nor physical nor psychic.

Pain certainly does stem from suffering, but it mainly concerns man in his lower levels of understanding, because the more man evolves, the less he is sensitive to pain even if he is suffering, and the more he becomes sensitive to suffering, becomes suffering itself.

The ordinary man is only conscious of his pain and not his suffering. The average evolved man (initiated at levels 1.5 to 2.5) has more awareness of his suffering through his pain that he cannot forget. Certainly, this pain makes him evolve but in a sporadic fashion and often very slowly, man having opted for pain rather than suffering.

Afterwards as the suffering becomes more intense, the more evolved man becomes aware of it and attempts to understand it even if he has no pain. He knows that this suffering will be permanent as long as he will not have understood its origin, which lies beyond terrestrial and atmic origins. It concerns his Spirit having become more alert to its presence and becoming more present in his life. His Spirit suffers as it tries to shake off the threads linking it to the world of terrestrial Souls, since it knows that this suffering concerns an aspect of evolution that is not only planetary but cosmic as well. Beyond this suffering exists a whole other condition that is neither suffering nor absence of suffering.

The New Psychology

In the coming era, mutual aid will be the keynote, because the difficulties, the setbacks, the lies, will be legion and in order to disentangle the inner jumble, man will need his equals to stay balanced. As much as some will unbalance others, some will have the opposite task. They will be people who are solid on the inside having known how to integrate Ray 6 in their past incarnations and who are increasingly able to integrate the energy of Ray 7 and to see the traps and illusions of this Ray.

The psychology of the Aquarian age will be a great help because it will unite all dimensions of man. It will look at the lacunas and allow man to resolve them by changing, within himself, certain destructive patterns to his advancement. This psychology will be more efficient because it is less centered on the ego and the mental aspect of man. It will be scientific, since the era of Ray 7 will allow an extraordinary scientific apogee.

However the new psychology will not ignore the heart, as is the case today. It will treat man as a whole by not trying to control his emotions in a logical and methodical fashion.

Science is on the verge of discovering the importance of the astral body, which although affected by the mental, is entirely independent from it. This body has it own drives that are not controlled by the chemical brain, but by a gland directly related to the germ atom. From here, we have the development of the astral body starting at conception, which engenders the emotions that allow man to be a complete being of which the inner range is played out in several notes - etheric, astral and mental.

Beyond this stage, man is no longer a man, but a cosmic being who will have known how to integrate the basest thoughts; the most difficult that a being can integrate. This is what makes him so complete, so unique.

Doubt

It is futile for man to try to understand the different modalities of suffering as long as he has not successfully stepped beyond certain initiatory doors allowing phenomenal openings of Consciousness in regards to what he now is and to what he will become in the near future.

Man is not aware of the origin of his essence, because he is unaware of the source of his suffering that does not come from the Soul nor from his essence, but that comes from a condition linked to this essence. Man is far from imagining what he is because he is constantly doubting himself in the negative aspect of the term. He doubts himself, doubts what he does, doubts his environment, as he doubts the existence of God.

These doubts bring unnecessary suffering of which man has a difficult time detaching himself. In a sense, man is attached to his suffering, since he loves the sensation that it procures, thereby confirming that he has a right to doubt when in fact it is false. Cease doubting and you will cease this suffering linked to doubt.

Man, the Source of His Own Suffering

There are few people who succeed in living their lives fully. Most people are subjected to life because they do not understand it. They do not understand that the essential goal of all existence is to arrive at being perfect in this world where nothing is perfect.

Man likes his imperfection, which serves as an outlet for his unreal suffering. He rests on this imperfection under the pretext that it is the source of his suffering when in fact it is totally false. Man's suffering comes in part from his own ignorance of certain laws. From the point of view of the Soul, this suffering is superficial. However, when man suffers because of his authentic suffering linked to his Soul, and afterwards his Spirit, he respects certain conditions that make him a being apart in order that later on he will become a being belonging completely to the Cosmos.

Man, when he will no longer be man but Spirit in his Consciousness, will become the source of his own suffering because he will have understood that suffering is nothing but the symbol allowing him to accede to a state in which neither suffering nor existence through this suffering will be possible. There will be no karma, no wisdom, no offering of oneself, because all these cosmic lies will no longer be necessary. Man will become a conscious light without a link to the plane of existence to which he is presently attached.

This plane of existence that keeps man a prisoner of the earth's gravity and that has repercussions on all levels will no longer have a reason for being for him because he will have subjected his Consciousness to something greater that has no link with his own present existence, tiny facet of his Reality, which develops through successful reincarnations and this means that his being expands through these existences.

He is certainly something else and one day his Consciousness will realize it. Man is but at the beginning of his real existence which is infinite as is God. Are we a dream of God? We are our own dream who dreams not of God but of God's dream, through his own dream. Who dreams of whom? Who is who? Our cosmic reality is not a dream, only our earthly existence is such.

Personal Commentaries by the Tibetan

Man always surprises me by his strength and his endurance, but his lack of heart, his coldness and his cruelty surprise me even more. It happens that even in my function as Master, I experience moments of immense sorrow, of temporary desperation, even if I never lose hope. I am, even though my essence is increasingly divine. Man and his cruelty create here in my monastery, emotional disorders among the monks of which I am in charge. These physical cruelties bring suffering, but attacking the psyche is worse. At times, man seems to be without a Soul, that is how great his cruelty is and his detachment from the real world that includes not only the plane of the form, but also other planes such as the atmic plane to which some people seem allergic. I cannot deal harshly with those who are not my students, I can only but endure their presence and negative influence and survive.

Some make our battles worthwhile in order that the best in man be cultivated and that it be exposed to the light of day. You, your Master and your group (at least most of your group) are part of this. Blessed be.

Life Conditions on Earth

There is no doubt that man evolves through a process that will one day lead him to his own victory, which really isn't one since man has already succeeded in part of his victory by living on this planet, and completing the work he came here to accomplish will only be the logical conclusion of his destiny.

Conditions here are painful but effective. They allow Spirit to refine its Consciousness, to polish it by giving it a complexity in the various facets that constitute it. Spirit is a divine energy, certainly, but incomplete from the point of view of experiences and this sometimes makes it a scintillating light that lacks stability and strength.

The man whose Spirit is attached to the earthly experience cannot but help accomplish his destiny according to Spirit, which is but the vehicle of something much larger, more perfect, but that is still thousands of years away from the Consciousness of God, who in fact does not possess any since he does not need it.

In fact, Consciousness is an invention of Spirit linked to man, in order to allow him a better evolutionary path. Consciousness is like a chimera but useful at this time for the destiny of humanity, who without it would be lost.

Existential Doubt Experienced by Man

Existential doubt as experienced by man is in fact a facade hiding the true nature of his psychic disarray towards that which he must now experience and that which he has experienced.

This doubt is but the illusory point in which his small consciousness oscillates between that which he must do, that which he should have done, and that which has been done. It implies that a step back would be disastrous and that the step forward, even if necessary, is inconceivable since the individual lacks will, energy and a just vision.

Doubt does not engender lack of vision, it engenders the absence of vision. Existential doubt prevents all correct perception needed to arrive at Consciousness in order that the energy of the Soul can accomplish its work through the personality of the individual.

It has nothing in common with the doubt that protects man against temptations, sometimes troubling, engendered by the unconscious desire of all men to arrive at a chaotic state of superficial well-being that engenders suffering and disillusionment.

Authentic doubt leads to the light of the Soul, whereas existential doubt, although necessary to man in his illusory world of form, leads only to a laziness of spirit, which man must put aside with wisdom and discernment.

Removing the belief of this doubt too early on may cause harm to the psychic development of the ordinary man who will have to get rid of it later on, in order to arrive at his maturity, since this doubt confirms his existence, whereas for us, it simply expresses the incapacity of man to face his own nature, his own destiny.

Man is his own enigma of which he must resolve the mystery with patience and intelligence, since the mystery confirms to him his existence, whereas for us, it simply expresses the incapacity of man to face his own nature, his own destiny.

Occult Obedience

Occult obedience demands of the man of good, a forgetting of oneself and a temporary negation of the inner dilemma that links him to the rest of suffering humanity.

The man of good who accomplishes without regards to himself or to the coming results, a difficult work that is demanded by the Great White Hierarchy, can accomplish much for the advancement of humanity. This advancement does not always concern him directly, since the forgetting of oneself often implies a temporary delay, a sacrifice of his own advancement.

He works for the good of all, forgetting himself so that more light can reach, with wisdom, his brothers and sisters on the path. All the peoples of the planet journey at their own rhythm, their own fashion. The man of good attempts to guide them through the subtle meanderings of their mirages that blind their vision and their actions.

Occult obedience is a duty that all man of good is offered in virtue of the occult laws that oblige him to expose himself as a disciple who is accepted in the white brotherhood that heads all of humanity on the 7th plane of Consciousness at the atmic level, or if you prefer, the 7th level of the atmic plane. This white brotherhood oversees the good development of psychic powers allowing the disciple to accomplish efficient work far from the indiscreet looks of his brothers. This work is done in the shadows but has precise and specific effects on the physical level. Only those who have adequately survived certain initiations, such as the fifth and the fourth (more restrictive numbers), can accede to this plane at will in order to accomplish their duty.

Man's Instinct

There was a time when man was dominated by his instincts. He built his life, surviving thanks to his instincts that allowed him to build a solid base in the material world in which he now evolves with much ease.

The time has come in which man must not just let go of his instincts but use them with wisdom and discernment. Instinct must become an intelligent tool in order to allow him to evolve in the three worlds including the subjective as well as the objective.

Instinct is different than intuition, which is more refined and more accurate in its interpretations. There again, man must be vigilant because intuition can be veiled or tinted by man's desire to grab a part of the universe that does not belong to him. Intuition is magic, instinct is animalistic and "basic".

Intuition comes from the higher senses, instinct comes from a mechanical process purely chemical, and directly related to man's ego. The instinct is the intimate friend of the ego, whereas it is not the case with intuition, which at times undresses the ego in order to catch a glimpse of its most terrifying aspects, those that dominate man.

Instinct must become a good servant and intuition must become a powerful tool that will allow man to better move around in the different worlds, the different planes to which he is and will be subjected to in the course of the lives that he must "live" in this universe, which is presently his.

Intuition is cultivated and isn't given to man as is the case with instinct. Intuition isn't a gift, it is simply the logical consequence of the psychic development of man that leads him to go beyond himself and to no longer depend on the logic of things.

Intuition is misunderstood; I would even say that it is the enemy of Ray 5. Ray 6 was dominated by instinct, which attempted to take possession of intuition but without real success. Through Ray 6, intuition became more refined but without becoming a loyal friend for the evolution of man. Even though instinct is increasingly dominated by man's psyche, it will always try to retain a hold on man due to his fear, which is his "leitmotif".

The Different Planes of Consciousness

We will now discuss the different planes of Consciousness to which man is subjected in order to perfect his evolution on this planet. The first planes are related as much to his psychic destiny as they are to the etheric and emotional. They are the basis of his apprenticeship on this planet.

By touching the superior planes, which begin with the mental, man prepares his destiny outside of this system, beyond the limits linked to human planetary conditions.

The first plane deals with the physical-etheric aspect and it is divided in ten sub-planes of which the last three prepare man to move to the next plane.

Physical-Etheric Plane

The physical-etheric plane relates to the down-to-earth aspect of the human being's evolution and encompasses the primitive instinctual aspect of man. It allows the maximum development of the physical cells. It is, in the first place, the perfection of the muscular-skeletal system, followed by the nervous system, as it passes through the etheric system, glandular system, and the mental system acquired via a more developed brain, the limbic system as well as the sympathetic and parasympathetic systems that pairs up to the glandular and nervous aspects.

Through this process of perfecting himself man prepares the tool, that is his physical body, to become increasingly able to perform with the cells that constitute it. Man is a cellular being, most certainly, but above all atomic, which links him directly to another plane, that of the atmic plane where the contact with the Soul becomes truly possible.

Let's get back to the cells of man (atomic). They contain his past, lived here and elsewhere in other systems and potentially contain his future. Man's responsibility is to condense and to materialize this future potential in his cells thanks to lived experiences that activate the cells and fill them with a sequential energy that in no way concerns the memory of man.

That which we call cellular memory is in fact a series of polarized or qualified atoms according to certain information received through these experiences. Reading this "data" means decoding the past in creative imagery sequences that contain not the ordinary memory, which can falsify the experiences as they were truly lived, but a memory containing a series of authentic facts thanks to which man can become a perfect being in this planetary system, by assimilating them.

Through this plane, man learns how to manage his material existence and this will allow him to acquire a solid base to anchor himself in matter. This "anchoring" will allow him to accomplish his destiny by the means of the physical world of this planet that repulses the beings evolving in other systems other than our own.

It is said that we have all of infinity to evolve, which is partly true, but those who evolve thanks to more difficult systems, such as ours, evolve due to the fact that this infinity is relative since they desire that others awaken in turn through the awakening of their own Consciousness. Their awakening therefore implies eternity minus a day so that this day can serve the good of another.

This first phase of apprenticeship is crucial and important because if the physical-etheric system possesses a lacuna, man will not accede to a higher level of information because he will not be able to correctly decode the events that are occurring around him or worse, he will not be able to transmit any valuable information coming from the higher planes. Man must be solid in his infinitely small in order to become solid in his infinitely large.

The Emotional Plane

The emotional plane relates to the emotional aspect that man must learn to manage correctly. Emotions color lived experiences and amplify, whether negatively or positively, the impressions received from these experiences.

The emotional body is the cause of the main problems experienced by man. It imparts notions that push him on the path or diverts him from it. This body is a sure and efficient way to learn about equilibrium, the middle road in all things. Without it being cellular, it is regarded as atomic in its configuration.

The atoms that constitute the emotional body allow man to accomplish much more in less time, since the physical-emotional plane represents the bridge that allows contact with that which we call the conscious Soul that pours its energy with patience on the man to which it is associated.

The conscious Soul is part of the atmic plane. It keeps watch and leans towards man's personality which attempts to merge with the Soul. This Consciousness linked to the Soul is but a subtle link allowing man to connect with this other part of the Soul, which faces the Monad, whenever it wishes and desires it. This part does not have to be conscious of itself since it simply "is", and its role is to allow the fusion with the Monad in order to become an integral part of this entity of light to which we hope to link.

Emotions that are expressed and experienced by man do not facilitate his apprenticeship of life lessons. Rather we would say that they complicate them. However, this complication favors the exchange of energy among the lower planes, which therefore remain dynamic and functional.

Color brings a particular energy allowing the transmutation of certain atoms that are carriers of more and more atomic energies of the conscious Soul that transfers them to its counterpart linked to the Monad, once man awakens more and more. In this manner a bridge is built, facilitating the atomic ascension of man towards his destiny which, although being earthly, isn't so at all.

The Soul does not belong to the earthly plane; it is attached to something much larger that links it in turn to a cosmic Consciousness that is ruled by those we call the Lords of the World of which Sanat Kumara is a part.

The Sub-Planes of the Emotional Body

A) Concrete emotional sub-plane

What is most difficult and most painful for man is for him to let go of the concrete emotional sub-plane. For the one observing from the outside it is fascinating to see up until what point man becomes a slave to this sub-plane because this sub-plane rules the emotional body in its basest and most common functions. It relates to the animal in us since it is linked to the instinct of survival and is ruled by fear.

This sub-plane allows man to experiment a range of emotions that increase his capacity to understand them and to no longer be the victim, once he has succeeded in becoming master within himself on this sub-plane. He sees the source and can deactivate their influence both within himself and with others.

"Base" emotions, or concrete emotions, are ruled by fear, which is engendered by the ego, source of man's survival on this planet. Without this ego, man could not accomplish his task here. Ego is that necessary poison that taken in small doses brings benefits, but that taken in large quantities, harms the individual and ends up killing him.

The emotions of the "concrete" sub-plane certainly do not make an individual evolve positively, but it obliges him to face up to that which we call the inferior nature of man linked to the animal kingdom. Without this sub-plane man could not have survived since without the possibility of understanding the animal kingdom he would have remained a prey without ever becoming its master.

B) Subtle emotional sub-plane

This subtle emotional sub-plane is very interesting since it allows the union of the heart with the Soul. It paves the way for each step on this path that leads to the conquest of the little self.

Once man has succeeded in connecting with the higher planes, this sub-plane allows him to contact, in a more direct fashion, its intelligent and conscious counterpart that links him to the Soul. This sub-plane is more concerned with intelligence than with the emotions it conveys. Therein is born the intelligence of the heart where experienced emotions are not egotistical but altruistic; they are scintillating and bring a lightness of being to man.

Emotions are part of the joy of serving the other without regards for one's self. A harmony is created in one's being, a remarkable harmony that allows man to execute his work and to bring peace and joy to his environment. He conveys higher frequency emotions where Consciousness can bathe without fear. Peace reigns within the self and a feeling of inner freedom is obviously present.

The gaze, imprinted with a profound love for all of humanity, expresses a state of being in which everything becomes simple in its expression. There is nothing that is complicated, since there is nothing to hide. These beings are open books in which a knowledge free of attachment to negative emotions, begins to circulate. The art of the man of good is to remain balanced in the two emotional planes without denigrating one or adoring the other. The law of equilibrium heads the committee, thus creating a harmony that is rare where well-being circulates and an inner security attracts others to one's self.

Mental Plane

The mental plane is also divided into two categories or two sub-planes. There is the concrete mental sub-plane and the subjective sub-plane. The first gives birth to the other thanks to the efforts of the Soul that polarizes towards man's personality. It will do so concretely thanks to the subjective mental sub-plane.

A) Concrete Mental Sub-Plane

The concrete mental sub-plane relates to the intellect, pure and simple. It makes one intelligent but not necessarily wise. The concrete mental is a Pandora's box, since we never know if what will come out of it will be positive. It is logical, not affective, it is cold and its advancement questionable.

We qualify it as scientific although it contributes little to the science of the Soul. It is managed without intuition and remains constant in its firmness to believe in nothing else but in itself.

It has allowed man to be comfortable on the physical plane but all the while becoming more and more uncomfortable with himself. The combination of this plane with the concrete emotional sub-plane provokes an explosive mix since it often engenders damages that are conscious in man's unconscious.

This plane remains useful to the extent that it is mastered by a superior plane that will bring it a heart intelligence, which will allow man to go to the subjective mental plane, access door to the Soul. Man is to become and he will "become" once he will take his distance from this dangerous path that is science without authentic intelligence.

B) Subtle or Subjective Mental Sub-Plane

The subtle or subjective mental sub-plane relates more to the part of the mental that is mostly concerned with active intelligence polarized towards the heart (in the first stages) and then towards the Soul. It has no connection with Monadic influence, which is more Spirit than love.

The subjective mental sub-plane is therefore spun of love despite its apparent intelligence. It touches the heart because it is profoundly touched by the influence of the Soul, which increasingly integrates itself in the personality of man.

It is therefore to say, that this subjective mental sub-plane becomes a part of the influence of the man of good when he has attained his third initiation. Before this stage intelligence is egotistical, at the service of the personality, who uses it in order to become more powerful. Whereas after the third initiation, intelligence works through the personality that becomes more and more the indispensable tool for the Soul in order to adequately accomplish its apprenticeship, here, on this planet.

It is useless then to mention that this planet is influenced by an intelligence that demands to be educated in order that the personality straightens itself out and becomes a precious good for humanity. If man redresses himself, the chaotic future of this planet shall disappear and will make room for a more harmonious future in its form and more efficient in its dedication.

Time will become more and more precious, since each minute lost will become catastrophic for man in relation to his path if he does not quickly wake up. Time is no longer about interesting conversation, but needs to be a passage to intelligent action that will allow humanity to open itself to new perspectives better adapted to its needs.

This subjective mental sub-plane is an invitation to group work in order that positive scientific discoveries benefit the whole of humanity, since intelligence must become wisdom, and our survival depends upon this wisdom.

Concrete and Subtle Atmic Planes

The Soul has two faces and therefore two functions that while being independent, remain linked to their fundamental goal which consists of bringing the essence of man to its spiritual apogee. These two planes are but the first level of an authentic spiritual advancement, since they are the first planes referred to as "spiritual", the others being but planes linked to man's personality, therefore little connected to his Soul.

A) Concrete Atmic Plane

The concrete atmic plane relates to the aspect of the Soul directly linked to the personality aspect of man. It is from this plane that flows the redemptive energy of the Soul that leads man to correctly begin his spiritual elevation. The Soul guides him through the influx that is captured by the subtle mental to then attain the other planes.

Touching the physical plane is practically an impossibility for the Soul. It is man who has to elevate his consciousness towards it and not the reverse. Thanks to the concrete atmic plane, man unites with his Soul by energetic means that are qualified as temporary illuminations of the Consciousness.

No real and concrete manifestation of the subtle Soul is possible at this stage. In order for contact to occur, man will need to have attained his maximum earthly light and must maintain it in an almost constant fashion. It is via the concrete atmic plane that this apprenticeship is made.

B) Subtle Atmic Plane

The subtle atmic plane is the most important plane from the point of view of the Soul, because it allows the junction between the Soul and that which constitutes its link to the Monad.

From this side of the Soul, everything is overturned since all the concepts related to the concrete Soul are blown to smithereens, the Soul liberating itself from the part that remained attached to the human personality. It turns its face towards the Monad that tends its arms unquestionably.

At this point, man no longer possesses the same warm contact it previously had with the Soul. This contact becomes more luminous, more intelligent, since the link with the Monad becomes stronger, man reveals himself to be less vulnerable to the human condition strewn with emotions that sometimes make the Soul vacillate on its concrete plane.

The Soul is love. The Monad is higher Consciousness that may seem cold at first hand, but that in reality burns with a fire more powerful than the Soul ever could. At this point, man transforms himself in a potentially luminous "being" from the Monad's point of view (we will see this when we discuss the Monad). Man becomes increasingly conscious of the condition linking it to this Monadic aspect all the while experiencing an inner conflict that makes him a being less and less "human" and more and more divine.

The Monadic Plane

This plane remains a mystery for many of us, because just like the Soul, the Monad has a hidden face, turned towards its future that has nothing in common with the plane of the Soul.

This plane is an equilibrium point between what man was and what he must be. This coat, which he had left in the closet of his humanity, can now take its place, that is the place it has always held close to man, who is no longer man but not yet a God, even if he has all the appearances of such.

Very few human Souls remain linked to the planet after having attained this plane that represents a return to the source, because in reality it is the starting point of the fall of man towards the unconsciousness of his human incarnation.

For centuries the human Soul has lived in ignorance of its Spirit, which however nourishes it and gives it its source of life. The Monad is the cosmic cloak allowing the human Soul to convey itself on Earth as in other universes. The Monad is that light that shines in each one of us, hidden in the illusory maze of our humanity, accessible at all times despite appearances that try to convince us otherwise.

The Monad is what exists that is best in man once he is able to recognize it and can allow it to be his life. With this understanding comes the end of "unconscious" human incarnations. And here occurs the terrible choice of remaining with the unconscious ones or to continue journeying towards a destiny, which no longer has its place on this planet. Man's choice will depend on profound motivations linked to his Monad and not for his love towards humanity because at this stage love is integrated via the Soul and is part of the Monadic condition without being the Monad which irradiates a light that goes beyond love.

The Monadic Vehicle

This body whose origin is from the Monadic plane, allows man to circulate freely through different planes of existence linked to our solar system. Via this vehicle man has the capacity to dematerialize and to transport his terrestrial image anywhere on this planet as well as elsewhere in another system connected to our planet.

It is this vehicle that allows the ascended Masters to pursue their work here by condensing their energy contained in this body in such a way that allows them to pursue their humanitarian work. This body is indestructible except by the will of the subject to whom it belongs. He alone possesses the capacity to do so, because once the body becomes useless it must be dissolved and not destroyed, as the atomic power contained within is too immense.

Thanks to this vehicle it becomes possible for man to conquer his own space in order to render it in conformity with his will, a will directly linked to that of God's. Only a divine being can have the right to possess such a vehicle that remains permanent as long as he can serve his subject adequately.

If we begin with the principle that the Monadic vehicle is an exact replica of the vehicle of the Soul, but in a more perfected state, we shall be mistaken, because the two have very different functions. The vehicle of the Soul remains attached to the world of the terrestrial form and can travel through different planes, but he can never leave the terrestrial atmosphere. It cannot travel at infinity because it contains too many memories that keep it linked to this world of form of which we are a part.

Some have already qualified it as "double" but this does not really describe its real functions. The vehicle of the Soul holds us back whereas the Monadic vehicle frees us from our earthly limitations and allows an extraordinary fluidity on all planes of existence.

Each divine being has one without however being possessed by it, since the Monad is at the service of the much larger "all" of which man is a part. The Monad possesses an altruistic sense even more obvious than that of the Soul's, which remains conditioned by our evolutionary system.

The Soul is subject to the repercussions of our evolutionary system, which is not the case with the Monad. Without the Monad, man would remain enclosed in an evolutionary system without true expansion, since the Soul has limits that are fed by its electromagnetic system which is subject to earthly laws. It is only by travelling through the Monad, and being absorbed by it that the Soul can liberate itself from the vibratory context of this planet.

It is the Monad that explores and not the Soul who is condemned to drift in the astral and mental planes without however going beyond its limits. The Monad is without end, which is not the case with the Soul of which the destiny is closely linked to that of the Monad. In a large sense, we can compare the Soul to the ego, the Soul in relation to the Monad and the ego in relation to the Soul. As long as the Monad has not manifested in a very concrete way, its desire to take possession of the Soul, the Soul will make it such that it will remain autonomous without an apparent link to the Monad, which is actually the true mother of the Soul and not its father.

The Monad has a nourishing principle allowing man who hides behind the Soul, to grow in strength and in wisdom. Love will be given by the Soul, discernment by the ego, an ego having become perfect, and strength in wisdom by the Monad.

The Father is something else, something that upholds the Monad in its functional non-form and which the Monad looks upon with a love having become wise. It is part of the hidden face of the Monad and takes care of it.

The Father is the one who creates, that gives space for its form, whereas the Mother is the one who nourishes and takes care. We shall call that which we find beyond the Monad the "Principle" that governs and protects the Monad, even though it plays the role of the Father. We are far from that which people consider "God", since this energy is beyond all things, especially the "Principle".

The Principle

The Principle has given form to our universe. It is constituted of a particularly high bipartite frequency, which implies a constant double polarity. The Principle creates from non-form. It is whatever has always been and has therefore never been created. It is an inherent part of the "primordial source" without however being this primordial source.

The Principle governs our universe in collaboration with certain energies that we will qualify as complementary to the source. This Principle is the union of certain forces, which implies that it is multiple in its diversity all the while being unique in its function. It is the mix of that which we shall call energies that serve to regulate the cosmos in its entirety. Each part of different universes that forms the cosmos is composed of a "Principle" that joins the other "Functional Principles" in order to allow matter or the energetic substance, which upholds the cosmos in its entirety, to be up to the task and up to its destiny.

The Principle therefore governs the destiny of each planet, system and universe to which it is attached. It has no real goal but manifests the raison d'être of each thing, of each being populating a corner of the universe. It "is" all the while allowing matter, over which it oversees its good functioning, to "become" and to perfect its functioning that is not perfect other than outside of the principle of matter.

The Monad is subordinated to the Principle; it is its tributary. Without the Principle, that which constitutes the Monad itself would not exist. The Principle, even though it is beyond description remains an energy that moves about in a circular movement allowing "life", since without this movement there would be no conscious energy in form.

Via its movement, the Principle activates a succession of atomic adjustments to the form, thus creating the Principle that sustains all life in all things. The Principle cannot die, because its existence is circular not linear and this gives the source the possibility to transmit without ceasing its own energy, allowing the Principle in its turn to transmit its principle that qualifies earthly and cosmic life. The Principle isn't linked only to our system. Only its "qualities" are, since each Principle brings with its movement a particular series of qualities that need to be linked to the form of which it is responsible. Each Principle remains unique all the while being united in a common task. We have deliberately chosen the term "task" instead of "goal" since the "Principles" do not possess "goals", only "tasks" that they accomplish with wisdom and fervour.

The Principle linked to this planet

The Principle is neither dependent on circumstances nor does it "effect", it is the generator of that which is while not being its cause. It is that energy that allows all things linked to its nature to unfold within a circumstantial circle without however being affected, since this principle isn't governed by time.

It is what it is and remains unchanging in its function. It allows that which we call human nature to take form and to perpetuate itself in a world where the knowledge of self shines via the knowledge of Self. The Principle, although not having any sentiment, preoccupies itself with that which lives under its tutelage, since these "lives" are a function of its duty towards the All-Mighty who governs well beyond the Principle.

The Principle, although tributary of the worlds that are superior to it, will remain connected to the world of form as long as this form will not have accomplished a full circle, not to say it is perfect although in principle a circle is perfect, allowing all Souls who so desire to integrate themselves in this circle to be part of it. This is occult law, unchangeable and perpetually dynamic.

The Principle belongs to that which we occultly call "the great force for the good" which indicates that the Principle is a builder and not a destroyer. It governs certain forces that serve to balance the atomic systems, allowing form to maintain its function. Without the Principle there would be no defined substantial forms.

While having its source from the "Father", the Principle, in its strength, governs this planet all the while respecting the will of the Father and integrating a unique energy that characterizes this system. This unique touch comes from the Principle and not the Father.

The present Principle keeps watch over the evolution of this planet by injecting in its ethers harmonious sounds allowing the human Soul to synchronize itself to other notes similar to itself in order that the echo produced by its notes surrounds and awakens the entire planet, which will become a specific note, different than the one that vibrates now and that will resonate to the ears of the other systems indicating its vibratory change.

Each planet has its own note derived from the discordance or the accordance of the Souls' notes that populate this said planet. The earth will shortly begin a key note that will take us closer to the "range" necessary for our acceptance in a system more elevated in vibratory notes. Sound is just as important as light because without sound there would be no matter. It is sound that awakens and makes the atom of matter vibrate of which the song is heard and known and recognized in all systems. Sound unites, celebrates and elevates. Light diffuses, blinds, clarifies, but without sound, we in this system would remain incomplete.

The Principle linked to this planet is subordinated to a Principle that we will qualify as more complete in its complexity and that governs several other Principles similar in function.

This fundamental "Principal" which is the great Principle, all the while governing a corner of the universe, remains inaccessible to our human comprehension. We know its existence, but its direct application with our planet remains, up until now, unknown to us. It is beyond our limited system of thinking because in order to understand it we cannot use our physical brain. It demands a brain that is neither physical nor electrical; it would be even more accurate to say that it requires no brain at all since the brain remains "programmed" in its function and is a major limiting factor to the expansion of our Consciousness. It is sometimes worse than the ego in the positioning of obstacles in front of the path leading to more subtle spheres of activity.

The Physical Brain

Even if the ego controls it very much, the brain possesses a remarkable independence made up of memories and concepts that it keeps in order to stay in equilibrium. The brain lacks security and searches by all means to keep this equilibrium that it believes necessary to its proper functioning.

Man's complexity makes him a being apart. Ruled too often by concepts that he developed in the course of his psychic "development", he remains a prisoner of form and becomes more and more its slave. He is then of service to matter instead of using matter.

We are made of matter, but what governs matter is light and therefore energy, and this energy can be directed by the conscious man in order that it becomes the essential support for the transformation of matter.

The brain is governed by this energy, and man must learn to bring awareness to this energy instead of developing his brain that becomes without "intelligence" while being full of "knowledge".

This brain qualifies information and categorizes it making communication possible. It is the intermediary between subtle worlds and the world of matter. Its utility comes from the fact that we live in a dense world, a world of matter. What is subtle must go through the denser world in order to become assimilated and understood. The brain serves as intermediary, but the more it remains gross in its expression, which in no way implies intelligence of the subject, the more it produces distortion of information received.

The brain has become a cult in today's society in the same way that the ego has. We glorify the brain, study it in order to make it a god that dominates as much as the ego. The more we study it, the more we become its slave, since its complexity has always pleased man, has always fascinated him.

In believing that he is demystifying the brain, man mystifies it further by giving it an erroneous power over life and its functions. All is illusion and all that is interpreted by the brain is subject to distortion since there is nothing more limited than a brain limited by our small consciousness plastered with concepts and memories. The ego limits the brain in the same manner that the brain limits our expansion of Consciousness. The brain does not serve the Soul, it serves the small self via the Soul, since the ego is connected to the Soul because of the experiences it procures; whereas the brain is not. It captures images, shapes and interprets them. "Intelligent" beings, from the point of view of the cosmos do not need a brain, since the mental goes beyond this type of intelligence.

 Paume de Saint-Germain Publishing©
Division of Orange Palm and Magnificent Magus
©Publications Inc.©
235 Rene Levesque Boulevard East, Suite 310
Montreal, Quebec, Canada H2X 1N8
Telephone: 514 255-8700 ~ Facsimile: 514 255-0478
E-mail: info@palmpublications.com;
Website: http://www.palmpublications.com